MISS CRANDALL'S SCHOOL FOR YOUNG LADIES & LITTLE MISSES OF COLOR

Miss Crandall's School
for Young Ladies & Little Misses of Color

POEMS BY Elizabeth Alexander & Marilyn Nelson

PICTURES BY Floyd Cooper

WORDSONG

Honesdale, Pennsylvania

LIBRARY OF CONGRESS CATALOGING-IN-PUBLICATION DATA
Alexander, Elizabeth.
    Miss Crandall's school for young ladies and little misses of color :
    poems / by Elizabeth Alexander and Marilyn Nelson; illustrations by Floyd Cooper.
        p. cm.
    ISBN-13: 978-1-59078-456-3 (hardcover : alk. paper)
    1. Crandall, Prudence, 1803–1890—Juvenile poetry. 2. Women educators—
Connecticut—Juvenile poetry. 3. Girls' schools—Connecticut—Juvenile poetry.
4. African American students—Juvenile poetry. 5. African American girls—Juvenile poetry.
6. Discrimination in education—Connecticut—History—19th century—Juvenile poetry.
7. Canterbury (Conn.)—Race relations—History—19th century—Juvenile poetry.
8. Children's poetry, American. I. Nelson, Marilyn. II. Cooper, Floyd, ill. III. Title.
PS3551.L3494M57 2007
811'.54—dc22   2006038985

WORDSONG
An Imprint of Boyds Mills Press, Inc.
815 Church Street
Honesdale, Pennsylvania 18431

CONTENTS

In 1831, the citizens of Canterbury, Connecticut, approached twenty-eight-year-old Prudence Crandall, an unmarried native of the town who had been educated in a Quaker school, with a proposition: if she would agree to it, the town would help her buy a house in which to start a boarding school for young women. Prudence agreed, and the grandest house in town was bought with five hundred dollars in cash and a fifteen-hundred-dollar mortgage. Prudence Crandall opened The Canterbury Female Boarding School in the fall of that year, teaching reading, writing, arithmetic, English grammar, ancient and modern geography and history, natural and moral philosophy, chemistry, and astronomy. Her students were white girls aged eight to eighteen who came mostly from Canterbury. The school ended its first academic year with no incident.

But the following year made history. In the fall of 1832, Mariah Davis, a young African American woman from Boston who was the housekeeper for the school, asked Miss Crandall whether she could attend some of the classes when she finished her daily chores. Miss Crandall said yes. Then Mariah's sister-in-law Sarah Harris wrote Prudence Crandall from Norwich and said: "I want to get a little more learning if possible, enough to teach colored children, and if you will admit me to your school I shall forever be under the greatest obligation to you." Crandall admitted her as a proper student. Once Sarah Harris began attending, the white townspeople of Canterbury became very angry, for they did not want their daughters educated with African Americans. They pressured Crandall to refuse black students. Most white Connecticut residents believed teaching elite academic subjects to African American people would bring about social ruin. And the parents of Prudence Crandall's white students were outraged by the thought of their daughters being taught next to black girls. The wife of Canterbury's Episcopal clergyman brought Prudence the town's warning: if Mariah and Sarah were allowed to continue in the classes, the parents of the other students would withdraw their daughters, forcing the school to close.

Crandall had been raised in the nonconformist minority Quaker faith, one of whose major beliefs is that Truth can be found by the individual through direct knowledge of the spirit of Christ—the "Christ in the heart." The Quakers also taught that slavery was a sin. They believed that by "waiting on the Lord" one could come to know the will of God through direct communication. So Prudence Crandall waited on the Lord. On March 2, 1833, Crandall placed a notice in the abolitionist newspaper *The Liberator* advertising her school for "young ladies and little misses of color." The townspeople intensified their protests and intimidation, but on April 1, Prudence Crandall began her school for black girls amid a growing storm of rage.

In the 1830s, Connecticut had the most homogenous population of any state in the Union, mostly white people of British ancestry. The majority of Connecticut families farmed for a living, and the once-thriving maritime business—which included the slave trade—had dwindled to insignificance. Though most blacks were gradually freed from slavery after the American Revolution, the state did not abolish slavery until 1848. In 1830, of the eight hundred African Americans in Connecticut, twenty-three were still slaves.

In April 1833, the African American girls began to arrive, from Philadelphia, New York City, Providence, Boston, and throughout Connecticut. Miss Crandall taught them faithfully and rigorously. Meanwhile, the townspeople amplified their dissent. They ostracized Miss Crandall and her students. They refused to sell them provisions. They went to the extent of passing laws—known as "Black Laws"—designed to isolate members of the school community, force the students to return to their homes, and shut down the academy. Crandall was twice arrested, jailed, and tried for the "crime" of teaching these young black women. When the new laws failed to stop Crandall, her neighbors turned to other tactics of terror. They used animal dung to poison the well that provided the school's sole water source. The town doctor refused the young women medical attention. Townspeople threw eggs and rocks at the house. Someone even slit a cat's throat and hung it on the schoolhouse gate. On January 28, 1834, while Frederick Olney—a free African American watchmaker and agent for *The Liberator*—was visiting the school to fix a clock, a fire was discovered in a corner of the house. Olney was blamed for the fire and tried in court, but he was found innocent in just fifteen minutes.

On August 12, 1834, Crandall married a Baptist minister

named Calvin Philleo. Somehow Prudence Crandall and her students persevered. But the final straw came on the night of September 9, 1834, when townspeople surrounded the house, smashed ninety windowpanes, ransacked the ground floor, and set the building on fire. Miss Crandall realized neither she nor the Lord could protect the students, so the next day she shut the school down.

Change was rapid in the years following the closing of Prudence Crandall's school. But change always faces resistance, and progress is made in fits and starts. Most significantly, the Civil War was fought and slavery was abolished in 1865. But President Abraham Lincoln was assassinated just a few days after the end of that war. Crandall and her husband eventually left Connecticut and traveled west, at long last settling in Elk Falls, Kansas. She lived an austere life, continuing to read and speak on issues of justice. And she endured a difficult marriage at great personal sacrifice. But she achieved a measure of vindication for her commitment to education when, in 1886—more than fifty years after she was forced to close the school—the citizens of Canterbury petitioned that Prudence Crandall receive a teacher's pension of four hundred dollars a year for life. The petition read in part: "mindful of the dark blot that rests upon our fair fame and name for the cruel outrages inflicted upon a former citizen of our Commonwealth, a noble Christian woman, Miss Prudence Crandall ... respectfully pray your Honorable Body to make ... late reparations for the wrong done her."

The school building was bought by the state of Connecticut in 1969 and designated as a National Historic Landmark. It opened as a museum in 1984. On the day that it opened in Canterbury, a Connecticut chapter of the Ku Klux Klan picketed outside its doors. Yet it remains a place where anyone can discover the story of Prudence Crandall and a group of courageous young women who together braved extreme resistance for the simple, just wish to teach and learn.

The Students of

Miss Crandall's School

for Young Ladies

and Little Misses of Color

Henrietta Bolt

Elizabeth Douglass Bustill

M. E. Carter

Jerusha Congdon

Mariah Davis

Theodosia Degrass

Amy Fenner

Polly Freeman

Eliza Glasko

Ann Eliza Hammond

Sarah Lloyd Hammond

Mary Harris

Sarah Harris

Elizabeth Henly

J. K. Johnson

Harriet Lanson

Ann Peterson

Mariah Robinson

Elizabeth N. Smith

Catherine Ann Weldon

Eliza Weldon

Ann Elizabeth Wilder

Julia Williams

Emilia Wilson

I

The Book

Jolted insensible mile upon mile,
a thin, high-breasted, sloe-eyed yellow girl.
Deferential but wearing the latest style
of Paris bonnet from which one brown curl
has broken free and frolics below her jaw,
all the stagecoach ride from Philadelphia
she has followed the beckoning finger of destiny
toward the place where she'll shoulder the burden of being free:
I shall learn, I shall teach. The book in her small gloved hands
hasn't seemed a Bible to the inquisitive eyes
of her fellow travelers. Almost memorized,
it comforts her as she watches the changing lands,
a friend to travel with into this chance
to bridge for her people the abyss of ignorance.

MN

Knowledge

It wasn't as if we knew nothing before.
After all, colored girls must know many
things in order to survive. Not only
could I sew buttons and hems, but I could
make a dress and pantaloons from scratch.
I could milk cows, churn butter, feed chickens,
clean their coops, wring their necks, pluck and cook them.
I cut wood, set fires, and boiled water
to wash the clothes and sheets, then wrung them dry.
And I could read the Bible. Evenings
before the fire, my family tired
from unending work and New England cold,
they'd close their eyes. My favorite was Song of Songs.
They most liked when I read, "In the beginning."

EA

Family

My master/father sent me up from South
Carolina to Boston as a nine-year-old.
My mother's illiterate silence has been a death.
I wonder if she still labors in his fields.
His sister, dutiful but cold as snow,
gave me a little room in her house, below
the stairs with the Irish servants, who hated me
for the fatal flaw in my genealogy.
For the first time in my life I am at home
in this bevy of scholars, my first family.
Here, the wallpapers welcome me into every room,
and the mirrors see me, not my pedigree.
My sisters, Jerusha, Emilia, Elizabeth …
But Mama's unlettered silence is a death.

MN

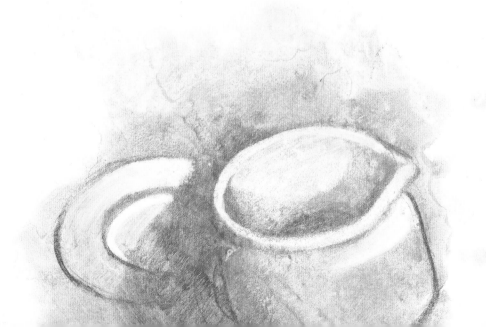

Good-bye

The mother who packs her daughter's valise,
tucks a Bible between muslin layers.
The father who shoes horses and fixes
clocks and other intricate things that break
saves coins in their largest preserving jar
'til the day for which they have waited comes.
See Mother wash and oil and comb and braid
Daughter's thick brown hair for the very last time.

Does "good-bye" mean we hope or mean we weep?
Does it mean remember all you know, or
come back as soon as you can, or do not?
Does it mean go now, or I do not know?
Good-bye, Daughter, says Mother. She watches
the horse and buggy 'til it fades from view.

EA

II

Study

Each day we study English grammar, spell
abdicate, alabaster, amplitude,
learn astronomy, geography, math,
French, and drawing in off-hours. Prayers.

After Mariah has finished her chores,
she takes off her apron and works with us
in time for our favorite book of all,
Peter Parley's Universal History.

"Suppose you could fly in a hot-air balloon,"
so in our minds we fly from our classroom
over land and water to Noah's ark,
"The Barbary States," Queen Semiramis,

to palaces, fortresses, sepulchers,
and the evil, the evil that men do.

EA

18

Fire from the Gods

I didn't know how much I didn't know.
Like Brer Mosquito on Brer Elephant,
now I know my capacity for awe
is infinite: this thirst is permanent,
the well bottomless, my good fortune vast.
An uneducated mind is a clenched fist
that can open, like a bud, into a flower
whose being reaches, every waking hour,
and who sleeps a fragrant dream of gratitude.
Now it's "illegal," "illegitimate"
to teach brown girls who aren't state residents.
As if Teacher's stealing fire from the gods.
As if the Ancestors aren't tickled to death to see
a child they lived toward find her mind's infinity.

MN

We

Colored are new to these townsfolk, who say
we have come to take white husbands, but we
are young girls who do not think of such things.
They see us horned, tailed, befeathered, with
enormous bottoms and jaws that snap, red-
devil eyes that could hex a man and make him
leave home. Though the state has said no to slavery,
we know how it happens with colored girls
and white men, their red-devil eyes and tentacles.
Our mothers have taught us remarkably
to blot out these fears, black them out, and flood
our minds with light and God's great face.
We think about that which we cannot see:
something opening wide and bright, a key.

EA

All-Night Melodies

An evening on the piano: ecstasy
could not be sweeter. Even simple scales
promise hymn chords, while six-note harmony
must be a taste of heaven's color wheel.
A fire on the hearth, the dishes put away,
twenty girls sit by oil lamps to read or sew
until Miss Teacher signals time to retire.
We form a blessing circle before the fire
as silence fills us with its constant thrum.
My fingers remember the ebony and ivory keys,
my feet the pedals. All-night melodies
unplayed, unheard, swirl in our shared bedroom,
meet other dreams, converge, become a sound
silent enough to convert every bigot in town.

MN

III

Lawyers

If not citizens and protected as such,
they are aliens and shall be driven out
from our borders as Turks or Chinese.

If the power claimed exists, then the law
has the power to send each white youth at Yale
College out of our borders as aliens.

This American nation, this nation
of white men may be taken from us
and given to the African race!

Can we call back oceans of tears and
groans of millions of the Middle Passage?
I tell this honorable court that we
owe a debt to the colored population
that we can never repay, no, never.

EA

The Tao of the Trial

Miss Crandall, you stand accused of knowingly
teaching colored persons not resident of the state
without prior consent. What is your plea?

The Teacher does not instruct. The Teacher waits.

Girl, has anyone been teaching anything to you and your friends?

Who taught you how to plead the Fifth Amendment?

Your Honor, I submit as evidence
of the alleged teaching of alleged students
this colored girl here, who openly reads books
and gazes skyward, who has been overheard
conversing animatedly in polysyllabic words
and referring off-handedly to the ancient Greeks.

The Teacher teaches, without words and without action,
simplicity, patience, and compassion.

MN

Miss Ann Eliza Hammond

I brought here, in a bag between my breasts,
money from Mama's friend who had bought herself,
then saved enough, by working without rest,
to free four friends. This woman gave me her wealth
of carefully folded dollars so I could take
Miss Crandall's course of study. And within a week
of my arrival, I was summoned to appear in court.
The judge ruled I'd have to pay a fine, depart,
or be whipped naked.

                Honey, the first white fool
that thinks he gone whip me better think again.
Touch me, and you'll draw back a nub, white man.
I ain't payin', and I'm stayin'. People's dreams brought me to this school.
I'm their future, in a magic looking glass.
That judge and the councilmen can kiss my rusty black.

MN

26

Allegiance

Teacher is bewildered when packages
and letters come from far to say how brave,
how visionary, how stare-down-the-beast
is Prudence Crandall of Canterbury.
Work, she says, there is always work to do,
not in the name of self but in the name,
the water-clarity of what is right.
We crave radiance in this austere world,
light in the spiritual darkness.
Learning is the one perfect religion,
its path correct, narrow, certain, straight.
At its end it blossoms and billows
into vari-colored polyphony:

the sweet infinity of true knowledge.

EA

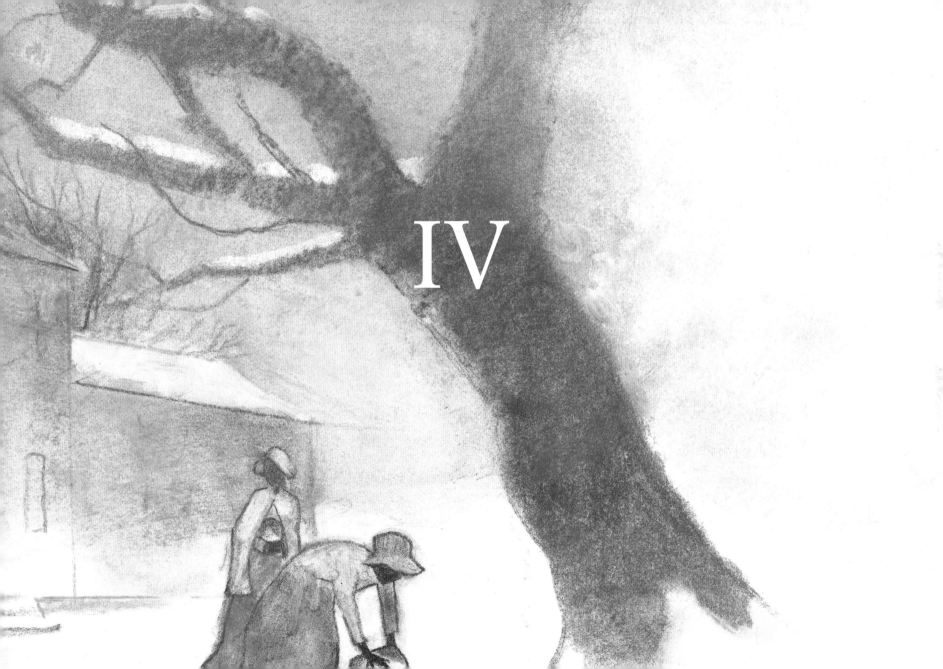

IV

Etymology

The filth hissed at us when we venture out—
always in twos or threes, never alone—
seems less a language *spoken* than one *spat*
in savage plosives, primitive, obscene:
a cavemob *nya-nya*, limited in frame
of reference and novelty, the same
suggestions of what we or they could do
or should, *ad infinitum*. Yesterday
a mill girl spat a phrase I'd never heard
before. I stopped and looked at her, perplexed.
I derived its general meaning from the context
but was stumped by the etymology of one word.
What was its source? Which demon should we thank
for words it must be an abomination to think?

MN

Water

After the shunning came the vile words, then
cow dung in the water well, fouling it,
so none for us to wash with, clean with, drink.
Past every dusk we gather pails of snow.
Mariah boils it, cools it down in jugs,
and so we drink until the water clears.
To show our faces risks their clubs and stones.
We take our constitutionals inside,
twenty girls two abreast in line marching
up and down the stairs, 'round the ell and back,
all windows wide open for cold, fresh air.
We thank God for the house we hide inside.
Bless the snow. Bless Mariah, Teacher Pru,
who talks to God and figures what to do.

EA

Unmentionables

Miss Pru's father hauls water barrels from his well
to our laundry kitchen, where we soak and scrub
unmentionables, then carry our pails
of wrung-out undies (growing increasingly drab
and dank from being hung to dry upstairs
instead of billowing in sun-bleaching air)
up to the attic and hang them in the dark,
where some of the girls believe a spirit lurks,
waiting, among the ghostly pantaloons
and petticoats, in the distorted light
of the starburst window. After several moons
together day by day and night by night,
most of us hang our linens side by side,
our march to the attic a private parade of pride.

MN

Hunger

The flour tin has been empty for a month.
No one in town will sell us anything,
no milk, no flour, no salt, no eggs, no tea.

The townsfolk have invented their "Black Laws"
to drive us out, keep everyone away
so we will stop our learning, leave, or starve.
They celebrate their laws with cannon fire.

We girls are not accustomed to rough bread
but learn to eat loaves made from stone-ground meal
and drink tea from the many different weeds
Mariah and Sarah discuss and sort.

In the cellar summer kitchen, salt pork,
sacks of kidney beans, potatoes sprouting
eyes we'll bury in dirt inside, and tend.

EA

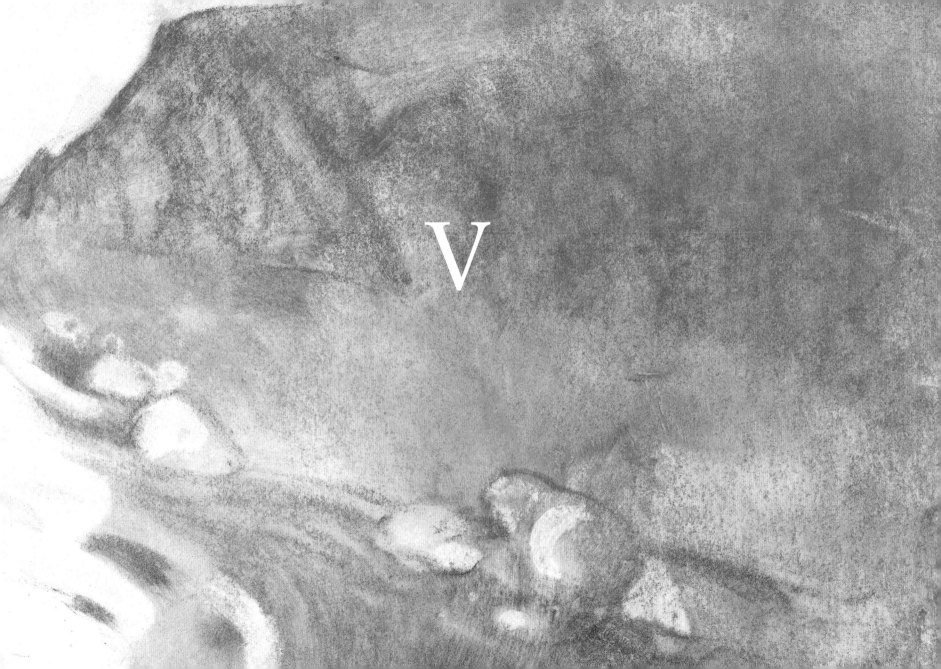

Albert Hinckley

Last Sunday, a white boy openly smiled at me
where I sat with my sisters at the back of the Baptist church.
When the pastor spoke of the sin of slavery,
the white boy looked back with his eyebrows arched.
I could read his thoughts, but I dared not meet his glance,
for nothing must pass between us, not one chance
for gossip to pounce with glee on one shared smile.
No one must think of us as eligible girls.

Waylaid by ruffians as we reached the ford,
our wagon was overturned. Our sodden skirts
weighted and slowed us, but no one was hurt.
Splashing to me, his eyes looking truly scared,
that boy took my hand. *"Let me help you, Miss.
From this day forward, I am an Abolitionist."*

MN

Call and Response

Students:
Having heard the bellow of fire roaring
against this house, we hear it evermore
in our imaginations and night dreams.
So terror operates: there when it is
and there when it is not, ambient, dull
and insistent, indelible. We read,
work, walk, sing; we pray to vanquish the flames.

Prudence Crandall:
I have never met souls hungrier for
learning, that which splits the world akimbo,
is hope itself in the absence of grace.
Who would I be if I did not teach these
young ladies, little misses of color?
Know I will never no never turn back.
My girls, we must sail above the treetops.

EA

Worth

for Ruben Ahoueya

Today in America people were bought and sold:
five hundred for a "likely Negro wench."
If someone at auction is worth her weight in gold,
how much would she be worth by pound? By ounce?
If I owned an unimaginable quantity of wealth,
could I buy an iota of myself?
How would I know which part belonged to me?
If I owned part, could I set my part free?
It must be worth something—maybe a lot—
that my great-grandfather, they say, killed a lion.
They say he was black, with muscles as hard as iron,
that he wore a necklace of the claws of the lion he'd fought.
How much do I hear, for his majesty in my blood?
I auction myself. And I make the highest bid.

MN

Cat

Eliza finds the black and white striped cat
tethered to the front gate with its throat slit.
At first she considers telling no one,
finding Frederick's shovel and burying
the poor dead wretch in a backyard corner.
As her classmates, she has learned to handle
what comes as worse and worse comes, like Teacher
and every person she has ever known:
to keep her hand to the plow, eyes to God.
Today, though, this day, this stiff, splayed creature,
open-eyed, spilling viscera, is more
than Eliza can handle by herself.
She runs inside, screams the news. Eliza
is twelve years old. The cat is black and white.

EA

VI

Open Secret
after Hadewijch of Anvers (13th century)

If your days swirled to chaos, wouldn't you turn
to someone on whose shoulder you could weep?
St. Paul says it's better to marry than to burn.
Wouldn't you choose the solace of escape
into the brief banquet of tenderness?
My widowed minister, with three motherless
children; my dear, whom my friends think is odd
(some even think my Calvin may be mad):

What is gentlest in love is love's violence.
Losing yourself in love, you reach love's goal.
Love makes you suffer, as love makes you whole.
Love steals your everything and makes you rich.
Love is both meaningless and poetry.
Captured by love, by love you are set free.

MN

Arson at Midnight

(Sometime in the late afternoon)
The mantel clock broken, how can you know what time
to gird yourself for the 4:45 barrage
of fists and hisses? Missing its low chime,
how can you count how slowly the days age?

(7:30)
Mr. Olney, a free black watchmaker, rides two hours
from Norwich. The meticulous repair
—wheels, levers, and springs catching slanted light—
lasted until supper. And supper is late.

(10:00)
On the parlor sofa, under a pile of coats,
Mr. Olney listens to the reborn clock
measuring being in meaningless ticktocks.
His mind's sky floats by passing clouds of thought.

(11:57)
**"Twenty unrelated young women under one roof!
And a man overnight! It's a house of ill repute!"**

MN

End

Upturned stacks of Webster's blue-backed spellers.
Broken slates. *Liberators* burned to ash.
Ninety panes of first-floor windows smashed,
frame wood splintered and jagged as tinder.

I can no longer protect my students.
Strangely, it is not God's words that ring
in my head as I search for understanding,
rather, words that I saw on a charred reader:

I must remind you that the earth is round.
Men and animals live on the surface.
There is no comfort in these words,
yet the fact of them comforts me: schoolbooks.

I am a teacher of colored misses,
but I can no longer protect my students.

EA

Julia Williams

Looking back, I remember reading
legal papers into the night (though we
were conserving candles) and finding
no intricacies to unravel in their
familiar and inelegant arguments,
Canterbury v. Prudence Crandall.
They won that time, but we were not deterred.
I went on to Canaan, New Hampshire,
this time as a teacher to other eager
young of both races. From the town and neighbors
came three hundred armed men, ninety oxen teams.
They dragged the school building utterly off
its foundation. I have twice seen bloodlust
and ignorance combust. I have seen it.

EA

We are both poets who have explored historical subjects and dramatic monologue in our work. We are also both Connecticut writers, and as poet laureate of that state, Marilyn Nelson has taken the opportunity to explore the state's rich African American heritage. Working together seemed natural given those elements and commonalities. But writing poetry is most often an intensely solitary business. Collaboration was an experiment for both of us.

On our first day of work, we met and made a pilgrimage to the Prudence Crandall Museum in Canterbury, Connecticut. The house is carefully preserved, and as we wandered separately and together through its rooms, we began to imagine the lives and voices of the remarkable Prudence Crandall and her brave young students. Useful archival material is kept safe by the diligent and knowledgeable staff, and that archive was full of scraps that would make their way into poems.

The next step was to spend time together at Marilyn's home in bucolic East Haddam, which she has opened to fellow writers as an artist's retreat with the inspiring moniker Soul Mountain. We spent concentrated time drafting poems and popping our heads out of our separate rooms to share scribbled bits as they emerged. We then returned to our daily lives and separate desks, finishing our poems and sending them back and forth via e-mail for comment. It was also at this stage that library research came into the process. Miraculously, we each independently chose different characters to animate and different aspects of the Crandall story to imagine

The sonnet is a hardy and evolving form. For a poet, writing a good sonnet is a great challenge. The constraint of fourteen lines forces a poet to be economical but not sparse. The poem must shift its energy in some significant way in order to essentially turn on its light switch, but in contemporary times that "volta," or turn, can happen in new ways and places within the poem. When handled well, the form does not call attention to its artfulness, yet it provides a scaffold that at best results in a sturdy, elegant poetic edifice.

Twentieth-century American writers took the sonnet beyond its seventeenth-century European origins as an architecturally balanced form whose object was to catalyze romantic love. Nineteenth- and twentieth-century African American poets such as Countee Cullen, Claude McKay, Gwendolyn Brooks, and Robert Hayden used the form innovatively. Brooks especially, in her sequence "gay chaps at the bar," used the sonnet effectively to write about an underexposed history.

The sonnets Elizabeth wrote for our book continue that tradition of innovation, stretching the form in new ways. Marilyn's sonnets are stricter, adhering to the rhyme scheme invented for the masterpiece *Eugene Onegin* by the great nineteenth-century Russian poet Aleksandr Sergeyevich Pushkin, who was the great-grandson of an African prince. For all of these reasons, we deemed the sonnet best suited to this project.

We next reunited at Soul Mountain. We wanted to put the poems in an order that would help clarify events for the reader, but at the same time we needed to make it clear that we were telling only part of the story. No book could recount every single aspect of this small piece of history. And in poems there must be room for interpretation on the part of both the writer and the reader. One of poetry's great strengths is that it invites readers into its world. Poetry refuses hard and fast answers and rather pushes us toward contemplation. For there are so many questions here. What kept Prudence Crandall motivated in her righteousness in the face of overwhelming pressure? What was it like for young women just barely removed from slavery to educate themselves? What did it mean for families to send their children far from home in an era when traveling was time-consuming and wearisome? Why did the townspeople display such fear and vitriol in the face of change? What did faith mean for each of these parties? In poems we explored these questions and others, and we hope our readers will do the same.

We offer this description of a creative process, which was for us unique, with the wish that it will show readers the many ways history can be brought to life as well as the many ways in which art is made. From stories, documents, walls that whisper, collaborative goodwill, and imaginative thin air, Prudence Crandall and her students speak today in these poems.

—*Elizabeth Alexander*, New Haven, Connecticut
—*Marilyn Nelson*, East Haddam, Connecticut